Turning dirt into jewels

poems
IMAGES
WORDS— JR/2003

or

Turning dirt into jewels

Jean Greenberg

Illustrated by Joe Rosenblatt

Wolsak and Wynn · Toronto

Typeset in Garamond, printed in Canada by
The Coach House Printing Company, Toronto.

Cover design: Coach House
Cover art: Joe Rosenblatt, ©2003
Author's photograph: Special Moments Digital Portrait Studio, Toronto, ©2004

Some of these poems were first published, in these or earlier forms, in: *Writual*, *Guide to Services for Assaulted Women in Ontario*, and the anthology *Brothers, Borders and Babylon*.

The author wishes to thank Joe Rosenblatt and Dr. Granville A. daCosta for their support, advice and encouragement.

The publisher gratefully acknowledges the support of the Canada Council for the Arts and the Ontario Arts Council.

Wolsak and Wynn Publishers Ltd.
192 Spadina Avenue, Suite 315
Toronto, ON
Canada M5T 2C2

National Library of Canada Cataloguing in Publication Data

Greenberg, Jean, 1942-
       Turning dirt into jewels / Jean Greenberg.

Poems.
ISBN 0-919897-96-7

I. Title.

PS8613.R43T87 2004   C813-5533   C2004-900445-X

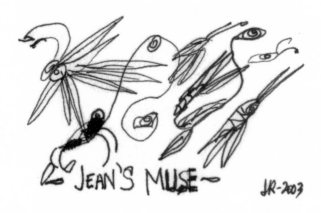

Jean's Muse~

JR-2003

Contents

NIGHT RAIN

Falling asleep reading Susie Moloney's
A Dry Spell, where the rainmaker
has just come to town and the banker
who hired him may fall in love
so far they have met in the cornfield at night
and he gave her a handful of rain
as proof and hint of things to come
the smell of rain in his footsteps
wherever he walks
an unfamiliar smell
after four years of drought
this genre unfamiliar to me
the codes for anticipation of the supernatural
       unknown

In my bed in the middle of the room
I am awakened by cool cool rain
striking my naked body
needles testing every nerve
the storm penetrating
my hot night window
lightning as close as love
and brighter
the most fun this old body's had
      in fourteen years

I get up to close the window
I must think of the antique lace
      I bought
to cover the antique dresser
      I inherited
I must think of what lies
between me and the storm.

SOUL!
JR 2003

9

DALE CHIHULY

Dale Chihuly in Jerusalem
takes a break from
building glass mountains
to visit Fairbanks Alaska
where they have the
best ice   six feet thick
from glaciers as ancient as fortresses
his eyes see ice
his brain says
negev   negev   negev
Chihuly likes that word
negev   negev   negev

Chihuly is not interested
in the origin of his thoughts
or their destination
he just wants to see
twenty-eight blocks of ice
each 8 ft x 6 ft x 6 ft
transported to the desert
there just was something about
the way the forklifts moved them around
in Alaska   something about
their whiteness how you could see
into them how they reflected the light
he just thinks a wall of ice
might melt middle-east tensions
no reason   just a thought
he has no reasons
he just sees
and does

Chihuly has no idea how it will end
he just knows
he saw ice
he saw desert

Crowds watch
held back by fences
it's not just the wall
it's the show
it's the klieg lights
changing colours
at night
shining into the ice
bouncing off the ice
it's the dripping
in the daytime
it's the Israeli
soldiers touching it
as they would the wailing wall
if they were religious

The melting wall
is a kinetic sculpture
renewing itself
re-creating itself
as it melts
as holes appear
as it falls

Some blocks melt from the inside
making lace patterns
others shape-shift
from the outside
others just fall

Chihuly misses one episode of the
sculpture show
the day he goes to the Knesset
that day many blocks fall all at once
like a child's first steps
the parent usually misses

No one knows how long it will take
in the October desert
Chihuly bets ten days
It's over in three

Someone asks
if he planned it
if it turned out as he
imagined

Just as I imagined
exactly as I planned
says Chihuly the poet
of ice and glass.

The gospel music I hear today
is not the gospel of my youth
now it is rock and soul, now they
praise the Lord with
long pointed
lime-green fingernails
glued-on
jagged elbows
jut out sideways
         courage is no longer required
to listen
         if you are white

The gospel music I hear today
is not round and dark and swaying
does not come into the
room of a ten-year-old white girl
alone on Sunday
the radio pulling in
call-and-response
the thirty miles
from the church in Buffalo
across the border to Welland

I miss the day I made my mother
drive the thirty miles to
Klinehan's Music Hall
Mahalia Jackson sang to me
with a blue-gowned choir
Mom and I the only whites
I got lost in colour and sound

Now
special bus tours
take Japanese tourists
straight to Harlem churches
and back in Japan
they sing in gospel choirs
study how to sound black
learn how not to be WASPS
with much success

Mom is gone
Mahalia is gone
I have no car
God is lime-green
Jesus on the mainline
no longer waiting for my call
can't call him up and tell him
what I want.

At 92
I/he missed the chair
fell to the floor
and sat there, sat
right through the long-distance
Christmas conversation
sat with
cousins, aunt, grandchildren, children
watching while at the other end
they knew I/he had fallen
but they still talked
and I/he talked back
I/he sat c-shaped
on the floor
my/his body as stiff
as our dignity.

At 87
after I/he fainted
coming down from Lake Hodges
I/he lay down in a stranger's garden
lay down in the mauve-flowered iceplants
so juicy and succulent
a better cushion than Dorothy's red poppies
and the sleep could have lasted forever
but I/he said
this is someone's garden
and I/he answered
but it's so comfortable
and I/he smiled
as one of us had never smiled before
we have our formalities.

At 14
I slid over on the wooden bench
with a phoney flourish
and a big fake smile
gathering up crinolines
in the high-school gym
as my boyfriend
asked another girl to dance
I wore the four-inch splinter
as a smile
the scar still in my thigh
not his.

At 43
he fell off the back of the boat
when my mother hauled it
up onto the beach
somersaulted into the water
she laughed at him
made him repeat the experience
for her camera
he smiled
not I.

CARRYING PIGS ON SPADINA
after Alexandra Leggat's This is me since yesterday

Did I see a man carrying two dead pigs today?
one hairless pink pig slung over each shoulder
heads down trotters up
slung over each shoulder like two fur coats
Did I see a man with two furless coats
slide into a Chinese barbecue house
on Spadina?

Did I see five women pass in front of him like ghosts?
Did I see five Muslim women
covered from head to toe in brown
see five women with white-laced black veils
glide in front of him
on wheeled feet?

(It was over so quickly.)

When I saw them was I on the streetcar?
Was there a lost old Hong Kong man on the streetcar
visiting his Toronto children
trying to get back to them
going south instead of north?
Did he explain in Chinese
and passports and pictures and gestures?
Had I already seen him twice today
on other streetcars at other times in other directions
on College on Spadina going east going west
going anywhere but north?
Had I already sent him north once only to find him
going south?
Had I found him an interpreter the second time?
Had she thanked me as if she was responsible for him?

(I am not Chinese.)

Did I see the old man going the wrong way
one more time?
Did I ask the driver to help him this time?
Did he say "That's my job" when I thanked him?

Did the old man start explaining yet again to another woman?
Did she say "Sorry I don't speak Chinese, I'm South Asian?"

(What goes around keeps going around.)

SPADINA   STUDIES
         PIG

GRANGE PARK, MAY

Black
man
tall skinny
long grey beard
combed straight
halfway down his chest
black
knit cap
black
dress pants
newish briefcase
maybe not leather
looking dapper
sits on a bench
drinks from a dark bottle
rolls up his pants
suns his legs
picks at newly homeless
sores

Chinese
man
red
baseball cap
black
windbreaker
pushes baby
canary yellow
snowsuit
on swings
bows formally
palms together
in Buddhist prayer
hands flip up and down

at the altar of his grandchild
laughs and bows
as the swing
comes to meet him
straightens up
gets serious
as the swing
moves away

White
woman
middle-aged fat
white
shoes
white
hair
white
sweater
beige pants
plays
tai chi and kung fu
waves
red-tasselled sword

Just the three of us
on a cold May morning
naked in spring with our clothes on
too early for leaves to
hide us
we take turns
watching each other
together
we watch the
baby.

PAMELA WILLIAMS, PHOTOGRAPHER

When she poses wedding guests
folds in dresses turn to stone

When dirt resurrects cemetery statues
stone folds soften

In adjusting her f-stop from life to death
she has made death softer than life.

SIGNS, NO PORTENTS

A squirrel falls from
the tree, breaks twigs. Misses me.
At shoulder height, a

seagull flies at me
aims shit like a heat-seeking
missile. Misses me.

Later, nothing happens.

SPADINA PIG   JR 2022

Bought myself deep red roses today
for my birthday
rushing into danger
thorns wounded my finger twice
my good red Isotoner gloves
prevented further injuries
sat back waiting for my family to call
the wind blowing the rose scent my way
no scent with my nose right in the petals
only when the wind blows
only from a distance

The building shakes, chairs slide
pictures of Cuba clatter on the wall
scent of the rose
so pale in the store
drifts across the room again
at the news of Hurricane Georges
three hundred dead in the Caribbean
in Havana a woman cries
on television
just yesterday a letter
from my friends in Havana asking
why I haven't written for a year or more

In shock I marvel at the power of
an earthquake to shake a building
five stories in the air in Toronto
and the breeze to blow the scent
of a rose across a continent
marvel at the power of beauty
to make my finger hurt
for days
aftershock of the rose

In other news today
a French man becomes the first person
ever to swim the Atlantic from
Massachusetts to Brittany
swims six to eight hours a day
swims 3700 miles in seventy-two days
only to crawl up on the beach
and propose to his girlfriend
the cameras roll as she accepts

And my aunt calls from California
to tell me once again
she remembers the day
I was born.

WHITE GLOVES

1.

There is a
maximum security prison
in Colorado

where inmates go
when no other prison
can hold them
cold sterile
white shiny walls
computerised control towers
inside and out
every door opens and shuts
automatically
eight sets of clanging doors
between them and the world
barbed wire walls and guns
waists and feet and hands
hobbled
in chains
covered in tattoos
they pump iron
bulk up
one hour a day
punch the guards when they can
for the other 23
nothing to lose
in solitary

where no one has ever
escaped
and the warden is a 4'11" woman
page-boy bob and pearls

navy and white spectator pumps
beat a song on
hard reflecting floors
standing on tiptoe at their cell doors
her heels slip out of her shoes
she can barely see in

she says
it's not inhuman
it's behaviour modification
and very effective

she says
she gets called a lot of names
most often
bitch

2.

There was a
maximum security prison
in Georgia
in 1910

where my grandmother
played classical piano
once a week

they said
Folsom Prison
was no place
for a lady

she said
her Presbyterian God would
protect her
if she wore her white gloves

she said
they loved those concerts
and everyone called her ma'am.

With any luck
for Kay Ballantyne

It will be like this
like falling asleep alone
socks on cold feet
like waking too hot
in the middle of the night
like taking off one sock
falling back to sleep
the other sock forgotten
waking in the morning
wondering
how it got to be like this

This is how it will go –
every five minutes a new day
every time my daughter
comes back into the room
I am happy to see her
all over again
today I have a teddy bear
to love when she goes away
today I remember a song from the war

My daughter holds a last Christmas supper
for days she makes all the dishes
I was famous for
torte cake with cream of wheat
cabbage salad with lemon jello
gets out all the cranberry glass
polishes more silver than anyone could need
today I remember how to use a fork
how to swallow
I can't learn how to make a wheelchair move
with my arms but
I still remember how to

put one foot in front of the other
she cuts holes in the wheelchair for my feet to push
now I can decide where to go
and have the means to get there
out into the hall and around and around
the wallpapered exit disguised
as yet another pink-flowered wall
if there is no way out
if I cannot remember
I am looking for the exit
I cannot be unhappy
today I remember my daughter's name –
Karon

With any luck
I will not be strapped in
a pillow between my legs
to keep me from banging
my ankles and my knees
until they bleed
I will be as calm and sweet
as I always was
I will go gently

I am one of the lucky ones
I stare at the poet
my eyes as dark
as a baby or a dog
deep unblinking eyes
that don't look away
that are not afraid
eyes that say
I know all your secrets
and I still love you

GRANGE PARK, JULY

From a distance
I watch a middle-aged woman
rise from the bench
where she spent the night
begin her morning ritual
remove the plastic sheet protecting
her supermarket cart
fluff up her plastic
philodendron
pull out a collapsible display pole
arrange the vine on top
so it cascades down
remove her cap from
her newly shaved head
pull off and on
layers of skirts dresses slacks

Just when everything is arranged and I get the message
this is her house she takes it with her
this is her world
this is her territory
here she is safe –

Just then right in front of me
a little Chinese girl
short bangs bobbed hair
frilly smocked dress with big bowed sash
leafy green branches in her heels
flies across the playground like Mercury
bringing messages from the gods

A sudden flash of light
startles me
only the sun glinting off the underside
of the wings of a dove though
it seems something else
and the dove cries look
there is no connection
except they're both in front of your eyes —

This Mercury
does not go into the underworld
does not rescue
this Persephone
does not protect
this Hestia's sanctuary

This woman is on her own
this child is not
(necessarily)
the mother of the woman.

Hair Nazi

Two doors this side of
the hair salon
I pass Ernst Zundel's Carlton Street
paean to Nazism

Every time a shock
a three-storey Cabbagetown house
now an eyeless fortress
all white painted brick
pristine
big black iron fence
steel door
a genuine drawbridge
a waterless moat
and some kind of
horizontal metal rod
hung from the roof by cables
can't imagine what that's for
don't see the boiling oil
whirring security cameras
watching me from everywhere
neat Nazi black and red trim
on the lintels and window sills
these barred and covered openings once
were windows
but never to Ernst's soul

What does it feel like,
I ask my hairstylist –
to pass that place every day
I never notice it any more
she says, but now you mention it
my day is ruined

In this baroque décor of
antiques and pseudo-antiques
the pièce de résistance
a floor-to-ceiling rococo gilt mirror
from an Irish castle
leans against the wall
antique chairs
masquerade as barbers' chairs
perky dog in our laps
canary in a huge antique wooden cage
(they bought the canary to go with the cage
not the other way around)
who needs to think of Ernst
when we can look at ourselves
in these cherubic gilded mirrors

Inside the sunny salon
we enthuse over the least little thing
a new scarf
wine-drinking etiquette
finding just the right greeting card
we discuss intensely
whether you need to meet friends at the airport
if they're friends they know how to get to your place

We watch ourselves talking
from all the mirrored angles
cherubs looking on
our hands flutter excitedly
we're pleased with ourselves
everything we say is important
at least it doesn't hurt anyone

Meanwhile over at Ernst's place
no one can see out or in
what would it be like all day
inside
filled with hate nowhere to go
no mirrors to keep you from looking at yourself
no windows
no frivolity
no gilt

GARDENING INDOORS
after Olive Senior's Gardening in the tropics

This year
I won't organise a community garden
this year
words will be my garden

This year
I will smell the words
feel the wormy words crawl
across the page
water them watch them grow

I will write about the
(indoor) tulip petal falling into
my shoe

My companion
the mouse digging in the pot
on my shelf
climbing up the philodendron
spilling dirt on my computer

This year
I will drink coffee from my
terra-cotta cup
with the green onion handle

In spring
clichés will become necessary
I won't need a smile for my umbrella

Mouse in Pot
2003

In the lazy hazy days of summer
I will watch my duck
sitting on the edge of the garden pot
under the shade of my ming aralia tree
his legs dangling over the edge
a red fish already on his line
my grinning duck will not be
as wooden as he seems

When there are no more flowers
I will look at the photos I took
of the tulip
before its petals fell in my shoe
and notice how much farther
the philodendron
has moved
toward the light
and I will garden in my mind.

shoE AND Rose Petal

THE BEATNIK CAFÉ

Open mike poetry at the Beatnik Café 1997 Nik Beat himself
presiding over the small airless room more smoke than I've seen
since 1960 Nik's wearing his beatnik vest his turtleneck his
necklace Nik's gonna make damn sure nothing disturbs his
atmosphere Nik's never nervous only his mother can make him
nervous she converted to Roman Catholicism from Judaism
nothing about her is right but she's not here tonight so Nik
presides even over the coffee grinder God forbid it should grind
when he's talking he'll shut it up quick Ron from New York City
these days from just across the street reads "Beatnik Café what
bullshit" Ron in his poem knew all the beat poets Ginsburg
Ferlinghetti Corso most he met on the street sometimes they
panhandled sometimes he panhandled I think I'll write a poem
about the Beatnik Café but I'm fifty-three and it's too late says
the poem yes my sentiments exactly I'm fifty-four and I think I'll
write a poem about Ron writing a poem I add up the years Ron
must have been a precocious panhandler but everyone else here
is too young to know and three old friends arrive haven't seen
them in twenty-five years since our children were in nursery
school the rest of the evening young people read from beat-up
Hilroy notebooks there is no more irony if indeed there ever was
and a young woman reads her first poem inspired by Bill Nye
the science guy she's a piece of furniture being sanded she's
never read it aloud before even to herself a young woman with a
cane reads about bits falling off her body we laugh she says if we
don't like her poems we can buy her jewellery just over there
on the table or her paintings which she left at home a young
man plays a piece about Gogol and the underworld on his
electric bass the same few notes over and over I'm accidentally
transported onto another plane ended by a minutes-old poem
from his tiny notebook where he's been scribbling humming
rocking back and forth a long rant about a priest in a schoolyard
entrails fingers on noses hands rubbing their own bellies
rubbing somewhere else too the words are tumbling tumbling
he's becoming incoherent yes schoolyards give him bad
memories a young woman reads about thirty-six people in a
windowless room silently wondering about each other windows

appear we should talk to each other is her moral endearing she's
endearing her notebook all scribbles and dog-eared can't read
her own writing my old friends and I exchange numbers they
thank me enthusiastically I say you make me feel my number is
a gift we leave trying to remember what one of us just said but
that was a long time ago at least five minutes we laugh our
children are grown engineers musicians poets designers I invite
them over I say come see my courtyard we can play on the
swings.

IF ONLY

If only
someone had told me
there were
new words and new centuries after
ozymandias and last duchesses
when at fifteen I wrote a
romantic story for school
a couple walking on a beach in Acapulco
holding hands at sunset
when in truth I just wanted to write about
the beach itself
how it looked, how I felt, what it was like
      to be fifteen
      to walk on that white sand
      to smell that air
      to see the pale pink sunset the blue Pacific
how intense the feeling, not just the sunset but this other world
      so new to me
      so far from small-town Ontario
when in truth I couldn't write about
the Mexican elevator boy, my blue and white thick-striped
      wool bathing suit, hanging heavy with water
      showing more breast than should have been shown
      in the fifties, the kisses, the elevator skipping floors,
      my parents paging me, the elevator still not stopping,
      the plane almost missed, my parents' anger,
the real story not the short story.

If only
someone had told me about
William Carlos Williams' red wheel barrow
beside the white chickens
and later about Purdy's rooms for rent

in the outer planets and no ordinary woman
dancing in firelight and throwing off her clothes
around midnight
and Carver's horses in fog on the lawn
and Rosenblatt who knew
poems are horses.

If only
someone had told me
there was poetry.

THE BARGAIN

for G.

Like a cat
I bring you
bits of myself

for inspection

pictures
sayings
jokes
my soul

but I
don't kill them first

and you
don't throw them away

I'LL PICK AN ORANGE FOR YOU, MERCEDES

You looked everywhere on your farm
for a certain tree that
still held an orange
this late in the season
only a certain kind of orange
would do
a kind used only in cooking
you only needed a few tablespoons
of juice
and a little peel
for the fish

You didn't know the English name
and I don't remember the Spanish
but two days ago I used the
juice and peel of a tangelo
in a lamb dish
and yesterday
juice and peel of two lemons
in a pot roast

And I remember you each time
I cook with oranges or lemons
you made food rationing seem elegant
you entertained me
with a gourmet mid-afternoon meal in May
you are both intellectual and farmer
by necessity
romantic to me but a curse for you
something deforming
this year's tomato crop
some unidentifiable black rot

One photograph I took that day had
just three elements:
part of Juan's green 1957 car on your lawn
in the upper right
(the word Opel, the immaculate grill, the Cuban licence plate);
a pair of Wellington boots
walking out of the top left;
a brown chicken
running out of the bottom left;
the three elements forming a triangle
movement as frozen as memories

I took another photograph of you
in a turquoise tank top
reddish-brown shorts
matching your hair
hands in pockets
in front of your banana trees

You let me pick yucca root
to adorn with lemon juice and raw garlic
and you ordered the fish
from a nearby river

All your goats had names
Madeleine tried to eat the
yucca as I peeled it
someone stole all the goats
the next year
and never learned their names

I think of you now
the academic
riding your bike the fourteen miles
into Havana

selling your produce
from a cloth-covered basket
watching out for the police
you support the Triumph of the Revolution
yet you cried in the museum
at the bronze American bell
the Cubans so proudly smashed
you had lived in Boston for a while
and returned home

I didn't see you pick that orange
but it came home with me.

FASHION MODELS

I pose
the flowers
take
their pictures

They don't mind
They're
dying
anyway.

SLY EYE
JR 2003

A black woman carries a
six by four by one-foot box
on her head
one hand occasionally
checking for balance
carries a big box
of computer equipment
in the other hand
This could be Africa but
her sure step coming out of the subway
in the slush
says this is Toronto

A white woman walks like a Rastafarian
a slow rolling gait
her feet turned out her knees stiff yet
her step like a lion
a man's walk
her wool winter cap
set on her head
covering dreadlocks

I walked that walk once
by association
by accident

She holds the hand
of a small child, her child
the effect of her walk on the child
not yet apparent
He's climbing a snow bank
I pass, see his dark skin, hear him say
"I'm climbing Mount Everest"
hear her say "Come down, you'll fall
inna road"

When I loved that Jamaican man
I dreamt my head was black
my body white

I long to be these women
to have this child
to be other.

POLKA DOTS I

I first fell in love
with navy polka dots
on silk shantung
in a dusty dressmaker's shop
in 1955 Welland

The dressmaker
was from Italy
in those days
no one
was from anywhere else
unless displaced by the war
we called them DPs
a handy schoolyard insult

I wanted a dress
seen in Vogue magazine
or maybe Seventeen
navy polka dots on white blouse
navy A-line skirt
navy bolero jacket
worthy of Audrey Hepburn

A tiny room
at the back of the dressmaker's house
jammed full of bolts leaning and tilting
every which-way
exotic fabrics from around the world
glorious disarray for my Anglo-Saxon eyes

For the fitting
barely enough room to turn around
my mother perched precariously
on a pile of bolts
chain-smoking
red lipstick staining the cigarettes
red lipstick pooling in the corners
gathering in the creases
of her mouth

I wore that dress the day
African men came to town
wearing long flowing robes
showing documentaries
in the church auditorium

Before that day
all I knew of Africa
I had learned from pink maps
and Babar
I had dreamt of grass huts exotic people
a life not to be found in Ontario

And now
at thirteen
I imagined my life
just beginning

And realised
not even the
Italian dressmaker had
African fabrics.

Polka dots II

I have always been partial
to navy polka dots
on white silk shantung
and African robes

In 1955
I wore one and saw the other
in a small Ontario town
– a miracle.

IT'S NOTHING, JUST A LITTLE BLOOD

1.

Red is the colour of
Chinese New Year
Christmas
Chinese bridal gowns
fertility
bright red for younger women
fresh blood
darker red for older women
dried blood
the gods like red
red protects the wearer
from evil.

2.

At Mount Carmel Chinese Catholic Church
in an auditorium lined with red pagodas
I have signed an agreement to
obey my tai chi master and
the Ten Commandments

Drummers practice for Chinese New Year
three lion heads are lined up on stage
ready for the dance
the master shows me
how to strike an enemy in the throat
with my fingers outstretched

Who is God? asks one display
a blond blue-eyed Jesus hangs, haloed
over a picture of the Jade Emperor
courtesy Hong Kong Bank of Canada

3.

On the street
jagged drops of fresh red blood –
a woman embarrassed or a man wounded –
lead back to the church.

TOMATOES

Sitting on the loveseat he
removed his shoe
moved across the room
as slowly as an accident I
saw once

Hit me with that shoe
as slowly as a car
hit an ancient
slat-sided wooden truck
full of loose ripe red
tomatoes
as slowly as the tomatoes
flew into the air
as slowly as the tomatoes
smashed onto the ground

It was over
as slowly as the empty truck
slid off the mountain

The next day
at my annual checkup
I hoped the doctor would
see the bruises
the missing clumps of hair
my nervousness despair shock
I hoped the doctor would
not see the bruises
the missing self-esteem
my embarrassment my humiliation

She saw nothing
I told her nothing

The third day
I denied it was abuse
he had a cold he was tired
he loved me

The fourth day
he denied he had hit me
I must be crazy I made it up

Two years before and one year after
threats humiliation isolation
worked as well as that shoe.

I no longer bleed like those tomatoes
I remember the shoe was no accident.

TULIPS

Tulips exploding
in my mind
in winter that
is all they can do.

WORDS, GARDEN —
J. Rosthatt 2003

Marta, I showed him
the picture I took on the
Frances Barkeley
the twelve-hour trip you and I took
through the Broken Islands
in British Columbia
the boat moving in and out of
sea-fog as the sea-fog moved in and out of
island after island
fog and sun continuously exchanging
in a square dance of light and mystery
the boat picking up kayakers
dropping off lumber for buildings
and food for the salmon farms
patrolled by German shepherds
on planks across the water

You sit sideways on the grey slatted bench
your arms folded over the back
looking off to the right of the picture
the red and black smokestack
fills the left half

On the right side of the smokestack
leans a young man
blond Nordic muscular
hands cushioned behind him
white tank top and black knee-length shorts
with red and white stripes
looking down and to the left

On the left side of the smokestack
leans a silhouette in blue jeans
a navy hooded jacket hiding his face
head bowed, hands in back pockets
looking out of the left of the picture

I remember his face so sour and lined
so old but not older than us
never looking at or speaking to anyone
on the whole trip
that man scared me, Marta
reminded me of Death in *The Seventh Seal*
I was so scared after I saw that movie
I almost got run over by a streetcar

You agreed to be in the picture as a decoy
I wanted to shoot the men
I thought of that famous painting but
in it someone looks right at the painter
and someone's eyes are hidden by binoculars

The contrast between young and old is obvious
to you and me, who saw the old man's face
and I can't imagine how I would react
if I didn't know but you and I
do know

I told him I found the picture
disturbing, even menacing
the camera's eye
saw something I had not

All I could say was –
all three are looking in different directions
all three are disconnected from each other
I couldn't say
that beautiful young man might be violent
that old man might be dying
or vice versa
You, I know, were pensive, dreamy, relaxed

Well, no reason to expect connection
no reason to expect any effect from
twelve hours of fog and sun and islands
you and I were strangers to them
as they were to each other
neither knew I captured him
neither noticed the other leaning
on the other side of the
smokestack

I wanted that sense of isolation partly but
mostly I just liked the composition
I was only interested in what my eyes saw
but the camera saw something different

Just now I accidentally fixed it
with a red frame with black detailing
the world again predictable
even cheery
a tourist brochure

I don't know which I prefer
there might be more menace in cheeriness
I might be happier being disturbed
being on edge

Marta, something else I don't understand –
the men are the threatening ones yet
the picture looks more unsettling
with you in it
than when I crop you out

When you are missing
the smokestack becomes central
the ocean disappears
the men become appendages
of the smokestack

I think it's just about the space
between you and them
and the ocean

and the smokestack
        off-kilter.

Symbiosis

Back and forth
on the crisscrossing asphalt paths in the park,
a Chinese boy pedals his tricycle effortlessly,
as if it's a 10-speed bike in the right gear.
It takes me a while to notice the old man behind him,
pushing it with his cane never wavering, both acting as if
this is something they do every day, and they probably do. But I
have never seen them before. They go back and forth, never
stopping or speaking to each other, both
gliding in a way they could never do
on their own.

That same day
in that same park
I saw a man in a wheelchair
being pulled by his dog.

VERN CROW

Vern Crow
reclines on his Queen Street grate
looking all the world like
a day at the beach
reclines on one elbow
as we do on Passover
to signify this day is different
from all other days
we can afford to relax
let our guard down

Vern looks right at home
Vern is at home
a pink blanket covers Vern's legs

It's Thanksgiving 1997
Vern's on the news
his face swollen
from drink
or punches
a fresh cut on his forehead
from falling
or a fist
the left side of his mouth paralysed
from drink
or a stroke
or Bell's palsy
like our former Prime Minister

The CBC has cleaned up Vern's act
washed his face made it pink
for our consumption
Vern is looking good today

The CBC feeds Vern a microphone
wants to know what Vern thinks
about our overcrowded shelters
wants to give him his moment
though it's long overdue

Vern takes it lying down
with as much dignity
as anyone could muster
under the circumstances

Vern says
don't feel sorry for me
I've been on the street
for ten years
feel sorry for the families
with children
homeless for the first time. *

Toronto Star, October 8, 1998:
"The most recent death on Toronto streets
came last Thursday when
40-year old Vernon Crow was found
shirtless in an alley on a
night when the temperature
dipped to 7C."

IN THIS ORDER

Small white picket fence
brown earth
green chives
red fire hydrant.

City planning.

ALTERNATIVES

Poems
are better
than
photographs

you can
take them
anywhere.

Photographs
are better
than
poems

you can
hang them
on a
wall.

AMARYLLIS

Amaryllis
on my ledge

Strung up
by the neck
'til dead.

GARDEN SPIRIT—
JR 2003

KANDAHAR; OR, THE SUN BEHIND THE MOON

Toronto International Film Festival September 8-16, 2001.
No one has heard of Kandahar.
Mohsen Makhmalbof's film has been re-titled
The sun behind the moon.

On September 11
I have seen two movies by 1 pm,
on the streets, in the sun,
between the downtown towers
walking from one theatre to another
I don't see the sun go behind the moon.

On September 11 at 1 pm,
in a washroom lineup before the next movie
across the street from the drugstore
where I heard the news that
Kennedy had been shot
a woman in sunglasses
acts as if she knows me
asks me for news
must have mistaken me for someone else
tells me unbelievable stories.
Four airplanes. 50,000 people may be dead.
Must be mad. Obviously.
This movie plot is not believable.

The festival is cancelled for the rest of the day.
I don't want to go home. I will have to watch TV.
I will have to watch people jump from the towers.
I will have to watch a man dive, one knee gracefully bent.

They only let me see those pictures for one day. But
they let me keep watching planes crashing into the towers.
Crashing. Orange flames. Over and over again.
Crashing. Orange flames. People running.

Women by the thousands
abandon their high-heeled shoes on the street.
Running. Running.

It snows paper. 8 fi x 11 lives. Before this
disaster movies only had theory to go by.

A man in a suit
carrying a briefcase
picks up a piece of paper from the debris
stops and reads
while all around him is dust and
dust. I want to read it too.

I found fire-singed poems in my aunt's papers
after her death. She never wanted anyone
to see them. I read them.

Comedians declare this is no time for jokes.
The media declares irony is dead.

Osama bin Laden leaves his last known hideout
owing two months' rent.

On a grey day, I ride the streetcar past a
turquoise Jaguar convertible
parked on the grey street.

Kandahar is a jewel in the desert
says my Afghan neighbour.

Kandahar opens in general release
under its original title.
Parachutes fill the sky
each attached to an artificial leg.
To save her sister
a woman must reach Kandahar before the eclipse.
She doesn't make it. I wanted to see that jewel.

The woman meets a doctor
who treats women through a tiny hole in a blanket
strung up across the room
an American black man
false beard for the Taliban.
Makhmalbof chooses his actors from
"crowded streets and barren deserts."

Music plays
kite-makers are back in business
men shave in the streets
some women remove their burqas.

A black balloon rides the waves
to the shore in California
lives for at least an hour,
lives after I turn and walk away.

In real life
the doctor in the movie
is a doctor in Afghanistan.
In real life
the doctor is wanted for murder
of an Iranian dissident in
suburban Washington, 1980.

Big Bird appears on a poster
with Osama bin Laden.
One of them threatens to sue the other.

Al Qaeda fighters are flown to
Guantanamo Bay in Cuba,
interred in cages.

A fifteen-year old boy
crashes a Cessna into a building in Florida.
No explosions, no fires, just the tail hanging
obscenely out of a window. In his suicide note
the boy credits Osama bin Laden.

The death toll from September 11 falls:
2,893, down from earlier estimates of 5,000.
The death toll of civilians in Afghanistan rises:
4,000 and climbing, not including people
starving or freezing to death or
succumbing to disease in refugee camps.

A man escapes from the falling towers
goes to Israel on a holiday
says Israel is more meaningful than Disneyland
becomes a victim of a suicide bomber.

The weather on TV now in Texas –
first a green relief map of the United States
then a green relief map of Afghanistan
as if we lived there and life was ordinary again.

When will they resurrect irony? How will we know?

The Budweiser Clydesdales trot around the world
past one landmark after another
approach New York across the iced-over harbour
pass the Statue of Liberty
stop in front of the gap in the skyline
paw the ground
bow their heads.
I cry for the first time
grateful to be manipulated.
Babylon O Babylon.

A documentary in February.
Firefighters inside the towers before they fall
grey chaos inches thick
every 30 seconds a loud thump outside
no one is allowed out the front door.
The man with the bent leg is diving onto the sidewalk.
Over and over again.

110 storeys became 100 feet in an instant.
Lives compressed, pulverised.
Months of digging make the pile a hole.
Looking for body parts, yes, for parts of lives,
and for 4,000 pounds of heroin
and a million dollars in gold and silver.

Tidal waves consume New York skyscrapers in a movie.
Since reality changed, even cheap special effects look real.
My stomach turns, would not have turned before, turns
even as I write.

The black woman wearing a miniskirt
and thick yellow-grey dust
becomes a minstrel show
known around the world as the dust lady
never leaves her apartment anymore
loses custody of her daughter
constantly worries about the odds of
dying in a disaster. Her name is
Marcia Borders.

A white woman without a name living nearby
a collector of addictions so she can write
confessional memoirs
tells an interviewer it was all so boring
cleaned the dust out of her apartment
and that was that.

On March 11,
two beams of light replace the towers.
Stairway to heaven.

I remember the man with the bent leg.
The man who chose how he would die.

The pale tulips I bought yesterday
turned orange today tinged with yellow
turquoise throats, black stamens.
They make me want to caress them, to hold on.

ALMOST HAIKU

That certain way
the sharp sun glints off leaves
planning to turn bronze
only in October.

In November
rain slides sideways
under my umbrella
disguised as fog.

Desiring spring
I buy tulips
in December
forgetting
they won't open
without sun.

Woman on subway
white from head to toe
defies the city
in February.

Chinese toddler
wearing pale pink cloud
against the cold
staggers through the park
drunk on April.

SEPTEMBER MORN

These mornings. These golden September mornings
in Alexandra Park, some days a light fog
lifting. We do our Chinese exercises. Afterwards,
coffee before work. Reading each other
stories we write for the occasion, stories of past
love, past pain, the best and the worst
of ourselves. Giving them to each other without
conditions. Yesterday
you rode toward me on your bike but I saw
you on a horse. I saw myself running towards you in slow
motion, arms outstretched, a cliché
the only way to tell the truth. I wanted to run to you
if only as a joke but I held back. You
said: "It's a moderately glorious morning." Through the park
through the big old trees all gold and red and green
to the Lost Camel café, life as delicious and
mysterious as the words on the sandwich board
outside: "The damn horse tripped me." If we never
touch, if we never go beyond
this, it will have been enough for
me. Now. This September morn.

LA NARANJA

after Tamara Stone's "Loteria"

Six across
four down
twenty-four small paintings
simple bright
paintings of objects
/paintings of their names
        in Spanish

This is our conversation.
We point and say out loud:

1.

La vela
        the white candle
        waiting to be lit
        on ochre

El serpiente
        the green snake
        bulging food
        on purple

El calcetin
        the white sock
        the literary allusion
        on green

Words and images that may
or may not reveal
connections between the ten thousand
myriad things

FROG
JR2003

La rona
      the green leapfrog

La rueda
      the wheel

El ojo
      the bluest eye

A large triptych:

BEACH BALL
J. P. 2000

El rey
      the king
      the brown rooster
      the red comb
      the black plumed tailfeathers
      the sly roving eye
      the devil
      on turquoise

La dama
      the lady/the queen
      sitting sideways
      the green bikini top
      the bare bottom
      the sly roving smile
      the flesh
      on red

El mundo
      the world
      the red and white striped beachball
      on blue

2.

La naranja
 you tell me about an erotic film festival
 the most erotic film an orange
 peeled and
 sectioned
 in extreme close-up

La naranja
 I have seen that film

3.

You come to clean my office
I find a perfect orange on my desk
 the scent so strong it
 stings my fingers

You do not see me
peel it or
eat it. But you
smell it...

We tear the peel into tiny
pieces
suck it up in the vacuum
cleaner

La naranja
 making dirt smell like exotic spices
 turning dirt into orange jewels

La naranja.

FOLIE À DEUX

You were the one who told me you couldn't write because
you would begin to live in your words, you would go mad

But I am the one who lives in your words now, stays up all night
writing poems, dreaming your dream of me, the dream that
makes you sane and me crazy

I am the one whose body is out of time waiting for your touch
while you sleep easy with your woman and your dog

You are the magician who puts my almonds in a story, who takes
my words, my being,
makes me disappear and reappear somewhere else,
reflects me back as someone
other than who I thought I was, and I am someone
other than who I thought I was

I am the one who needs to keep a pen by her pillow at midnight
to find a way to tell you I am
addicted to your paper touch,
addicted to your sensuous phrases –
"I went back and drank out of her glass" or
"You rose to breathe my air"

I am the one who can't wait each morning to see what new
images you'll bring me, wondering
how I will be reflected in your mirror today, wondering if
I will recognise myself, or know if
those are my almonds being eaten by another woman who
may or may not be real, who
may or may not be me.

I'm sinking fast and I need to be saved,
saved from your paper love.

CHIMERA

1.

Come to me my love
come to me in the mornings
make love with me with words
come to me at night
make love with me in my dreams
let me wake up vibrating after you've gone

Only touch me, touch me
touch my hands, my face, my shoulders
hold me before I die of longing
for your touch
my tormentor, my love

2.

Come, my love, let me touch you in the day
let me make love with you at night when I'm alone

That first and only touch
your hand cupping my face
gave me more pleasure than I could bear
something ineffable between your hand and my face

You can make me blush
you can make me laugh
you can make my skin sing

3.

I am with you when I rise in the morning and write to you
I am with you at night when you come to my bed in my dreams
and we dream your stories together, but I can
change the endings

You touched my face
my skin leapt to your hand
and was cupped in such grace

My body betrays me
I wake up at night pulsing, not wanting
the sleep I so badly need
my soul calls your name

4.

Come to me my phantom lover
make a single chimera from two mythical creatures

Your hands on the reins
a flick of your finger on the paper
horse and rider interchangeably one

You held half my face in your hand
when I slept the moon was half full, and bright

You can make me love
you can make my soul sing

5.

Come to me my demon muse
strike at any time
just after sunset or at three in the morning
there is no such thing as time

Come to me my dream lover, my paper lover,
my own.

THE ALCHEMIST

You're my private hunter
I'm your only prey
you follow my tracks for days
sniff the ground
study my habits
eat me for dinner
my bones become your oracle
appear the next day
as stories

My almonds pop up in Sudbury
you drink out of my glass
a hill in Scotland moves to Florida
grass becomes cement
your hand and face replace another's
            in a photograph

You're my private musician
I'm your harp
you play me when you're ready
my body sings for you

I'm your Jodrell Bank
sensitive to all the galaxies
I receive your signals
transmit them wherever you want

But I am not your muse
I am your life-class model
you pose me
paint me
create me
in your own image.

WORDS AND TEETH

Come down off the page
                    and love me
step off the page
                    it's not far
from the ground.
                    Step off.

Steady. I've got you. Give me your hand.
I know you want to. I know you know how.

Escape into me. It's closer than you think
from there to here. You gave me part
of yourself – your tooth – already as detached
as your words on the page. I'll keep it
safe, but it's no longer you. Teeth and
words are no substitutes for action. I've
discovered what's stopping you. I know
your secret. You have given me the clues. Join
your tooth in my safekeeping.

Hold me. I seek an everyday pleasure I was
beginning to think was wrong. I almost
forgot my need to touch you is just my
ordinary human need.

Words can deceive and teeth can be anyone's. I want
the you that is still you. The you that has not been
yanked out, that is still whole. You deserve pleasure,
you deserve to be re-connected
                    to me/to the world/to yourself.

I want you to remember your everyday pleasure, your
ordinary need. Leave
it in your body where it belongs. Keep it for yourself
only show it to me.

AN ATLAS OF CLOUDS

Toronto to Chicago. Winter clouds with spikes like dreadlocked
sheep. The book you wanted, "An Atlas of Clouds", is not in any
catalogues.

In this inverted world everything is blue-grey – the lake, the
fields dusted with snow, the very air, so thin. It's cold where you
are, and I can't get to you. Ripples on the lake like ice on a
winter street. Waves or ice I can't tell, nothing moves from up
here, I have lost my perspective. On this street skyscrapers poke
out into the water like ice castles. A child says: "It was all lake,
now here come the buildings, here comes Chicago."

Chicago to Austin. Isolated clouds decorate tapestry fields like
the patches I once sewed on a couch I could not afford to
replace, the inside falling apart faster than the outside could
hold. The sun reflects off sparse clouds and cannot reach the
ground. I take these clouds out of the sky and give them to you.
But you will have to name them. And you will have to explain
why the sun can't penetrate them.

Now a pink river reflects the clouds back to themselves. Now a
thin layer just below, a gauze safety net covering soft green and
brown fields. Now we gallop, horses in a dream, over newly
ploughed cloud-fields. And I am sure I can touch them, as sure
as when I looked for God outside the airplane window when I
was five, looked for his beard flowing among the clouds. Once I
was seventeen in Switzerland and there were clouds every day
from September through December. In January three famous
mountains appeared unannounced at my window.

Now a private vertical rainbow: pale yellow to yellow to orange
to almost red. No purple or blue. But there is no rain and this is
not a rainbow, but the sunset. You would say it depends on your
perspective.

An orange wedge splits the clouds, creating blue sky above and a second sunset. And twice more the sun sets in waves of grey, blue, orange, the clouds ridged, clenching like orgasmic muscles. And my naked heart is a camera funnelling images into my atlas.

San Diego to Toronto. The earth changes rapidly from up here. The lines are clear. Fields of green, brown and taupe, then suddenly desert. The earth becomes a red beard with ingrown hairs, fissures appear, mountains stop suddenly in a line of snow that is not snow, but clouds. Flat reddish land scored by hieroglyphs, geometric spider-webs spiralling into uninhabited squares. You would give them meaning: I have my geometry, you always said. In the psychiatric ward you drew interlocking hexagons. Beehives, you said, and flukes: y-shaped sea-creatures able to navigate a maze they had never seen before, when fed pieces of other flukes that had already learned the way through.

The Orange, Part Two

I represent stability in your life –
a little coffee, a little tea, maybe a muffin,
some words on paper.

You wrote about making love with your spouse. I wanted
it to be me, me you were entering, matching your thrusts with
my breathing, in when I breathe in, out when I breathe out,
a little frustration to stir in my coffee. I am
your pal, your friend, your steady homework. But you
kissed me and don't remember, you touched me, yes.
You remember only your lips stinging from the orange.
I remember my lips soothing yours, taking the sting away. I
had brought you the orange. You opened it, ate the peel,
gave me the flesh inside. I said no, you deserve the orange,
what's inside me. I fed you, piece by piece, your lips grazing
my fingers. I was delicate, careful.

You said "I'm irresponsible when I'm crazy" and kissed me
for the first time. Kissed me, an orange section inside your
mouth, pushing it into mine with your teeth so sweet. I
bit into it, my mouth on yours, swallowing
juice from your mouth and the orange.

You kissed me and don't remember. I remember your lips,
your mouth becoming more insistent, mine meeting yours
more hesitantly. Trying to hold back. People were
watching. Your spouse might show up. I was
supposed to be the sane one. I wasn't
the one locked up. You loved me and don't remember.

Your mouth on my neck, my neck more sensitive than my lips
my neck telling you I can't stop can't stop don't want to stop.
My words echoing. Moaning, sighing, I push you away too late.
The guard says don't be so obvious, there are other people
here. Your shadow crazy, the susceptible one,
looks at us knowingly, makes signs of approval,
becomes agitated on our behalf, aggressive.
Who can blame him?

You said "You love me, don't you?"
And I'm the one who doesn't remember
what I asked you in return. You might have answered
"The feeling is sort of mutual" as you once said
"It's a moderately glorious day."

The second day your shadow crazy paces outside your
glass room, staring, haranguing when we touch, a
monkey king. The guards carry him away screaming. I know
you remember the first day. We both remember now.

The third day your shadow crazy is puzzled. He holds the key,
has seen you in your glass room,
has seen you with two women.
He asks – "What's your relationship?"
You answer – "Buddies."
He says – "It's a fine line."

And it's a fine line between remembering and forgetting.
When exactly does it slip from one into the other?
One day I'll forget, too. We'll return to tea and oranges,
as we have already done. Love documented. Documented love.
My words make you erect, but not me, not me.

There was a day when we breathed together with you in me
as I breathed in. We both remember not now not then, but
another time, another life when your movement in my stillness
meant something.

In that other life we were lovers. In this we will be friends.
No need to complain just as I don't complain
about having the second most beautiful smile
you have ever seen.

I just need to forget your mouth. Just need to remember
not to wait for an orange that will not be peeled again
in this lifetime.

VENN DIAGRAM

Loved by my tai chi sword I now move
in circles of my own making
no longer sitting with you
in ninety degree second-hand armchairs
a beaten copper table between us
a potential mirror behind us revealing our backs
to each other.

If the walls were mirrors behind us
someone standing in front would see
their true reflection. We sit, each
backed against a wall in armchairs.
Our non-dominant elbows can rest
on the table in the corner. Tea
is not the only refreshment.

The sword's circular flash
looks real from a distance
astounds innocents and children
who believe an old sword-carrying woman
but the sword is collapsible
can begin and end in a flash

I know how to let go of my soul.
And it is a bird soaring too high to identify,
probably a carrion eater, not a bird of prey. If
I had not told you this I would never
have known. I am in a high, dry space for now.

I never told you about my reincarnation experience
I killed someone in eighteenth century England
and was reborn with a club foot
my left foot.

I kiss you for the first time and ask
"Do you want to be reborn?"

But I'd rather be with you
sitting at right angles
reading your two-page stories
you reading my poems
than leaping in the arc
of my sword.

I remember the upward curve of a sword. I see
the left foot you told me about before you
changed your socks. I see the smile that grows
huge as the cue cards
under my mother's mouth
teaching me, prompting me.
I am tinder and ash.